STUDY GUIDE

What's Your Problem?

Discovering God's Greatness in the Midst of Your Storms

EMILY A. EDWARDS, PH.D.

Living Hope Publishing ▪ Midland, Texas

© 2015 Emily A. Edwards, Ph.D. All rights reserved. No part of this book may be reproduced in any form or by any electronic or mechanical means, including information storage and retrieval systems, without permission in writing from the publisher, except by a reviewer who may quote brief passages in a review.

LIVING HOPE PUBLISHING
www.LivingHopePublishing.com

Book design by TLC Graphics, *www.TLCGraphics.com*
Cover: Tamara Dever, Interior: Erin Stark

All Scripture quotations, unless otherwise indicated, are taken from the *New King James Version*. Copyright © 1982 by Thomas Nelson, Inc. Used by permission. All rights reserved.

ISBN: 978-0-9816709-5-9

Contents

Acknowledgments v

Introduction vii

1. Got Problems? 1

2. A Reason for All Seasons 9

3. Trials Aren't Wasted Time 17

4. Suffering with the Right Attitude 25

5. For Such a Time as This 33

6. Redefining Victory 41

7. Your Response Reveals Your Heart 49

8. When We Don't Understand 57

9. Forks in the Road 65

10. Muscle-Building Adversity 73

11. Want Hope? Stop, Drop, and Roll 81

12. Enduring with Patience 89

Conclusion 97

About the Author 99

Acknowledgments

First and foremost, I would like to thank my Lord and Savior, Jesus Christ. This journey would not have been possible without His direction and help. There are so many people who have helped, guided, encouraged, prayed, and stood by me through the journey of completing this study guide and the companion book, *What's Your Problem? Discovering God's Greatness in the Midst of Your Storms*. I would specifically like to thank my husband, Chad, for your love and support through this. I love you so much. I would like to thank Heidi Tolliver-Walker for her editing and help with these books. You're a blessing from God. I would also like to thank David Crass, Steven Brown, Morgan McDonald, Lacy Weitzel, Jenny Mertes, Elizabeth Gressett, Michelle Schuldt, Katie Brown, Kristen Brown, Karen Burkett, Valerie Paine, Kathy Bruins, Tamara Dever, and Erin Stark. Thanks to all my friends and family for your love and support.

Introduction

What's Your Problem? Discovering God's Greatness in the Midst of Your Storms is designed to give people guidance and direction through the Scriptures on how to deal with problems and trials. Throughout our lives, we face challenges that often seem overwhelming. As a Christian counselor, my deepest desire is to encourage others to find hope in the one who calms the storms—the one who cares deeply about our most painful wounds and our most frightening dilemmas. I want readers to be encouraged by the testimonies of those who have faced seemingly overwhelming odds and seen God turn to good what the enemy meant for harm (Genesis 50:20). Perhaps you're currently facing the greatest heartache of your life. If so, let the truths in What's Your Problem? and this companion study guide help you through.

The purpose of this study guide is to encourage you and help you understand how you arrived where you are now and how to get where you want to be. The questions are designed to help you consider why you make certain decisions, why you use certain methods to deal with troubles, and why you find yourself facing the same issues again and again. Do you tend to deny problems and stuff them under the rug, or do you turn to God and trust Him? If you are dealing with problems in unhealthy and counterproductive ways, this study guide offers better, healthier approaches that will produce a more beneficial outcome. If you take the time to answer each question honestly and thoughtfully, you will gain insight into your actions and learn how to apply biblical principles to each situation.

Although the book and study guide can be used separately, I encourage you to use them together for your greatest benefit. You may choose to use these resources on your own or as part of a group discussion. Allow the Holy Spirit to reveal weaknesses in your life and minister to you in the areas in which He wants you to learn and grow. If you use these resources as part of a small group study, let God use them to build closer relationships with others as you share your struggles with each other. As you trust and obey God, He will lead you out of bondage and confusion into a place of peace and joy you've never imagined.

Got Problems?

Several years ago, I was driving on a beautiful, sunny day. Suddenly, out of nowhere, dark clouds gathered thickly in the sky. Soon, hard rain slapped my windshield with such ferocity that I felt as though I were going through a carwash. The rain was not factored into my plans! It slowed down my driving, and I reached my destination later than I had anticipated. For much of the time, it was very hard to see the road or the landmarks around me. Throughout the storm, however, there were flashes of lightning that lit up the landscape around me. For those brief seconds, I could see through the darkness and confirm that I was still going in the right direction. These flashes of light between the long stretches of squinting through my windshield encouraged me.

Have you experienced dark clouds in your life? Have you experienced times when there was no warning of the impending storm and the pelting of the rain seemed endless? God provides an answer for your storm. He will flash His presence while it's raging to let you know He is there and that you are not left to fend for yourself. Let's turn to God's Word and see what it says about facing the storms in our lives.

1. What is God's perspective on trials? How might it differ from yours? How can this knowledge help you gain a new perspective?

   _____
   _____
   _____
   _____
   _____
   _____
   _____

2. At times, we are tempted to think that if God would only get in line with our will and plan, things would be much easier. Have you ever experienced a situation in which you thought you knew better than God did? Describe it.

   _____
   _____
   _____
   _____
   _____
   _____
   _____
   _____

3. Study John 5:5–6. At first it seems odd that Jesus would ask someone who had been sick for thirty-eight years if he wanted to get well. But don't we need to answer the same question sometimes? We often find it easier to stay where we are and hope things will get better than to actually *do* something different. Intentionally implementing change is hard. How about you? When you encounter problems, are you comfortable trying to solve the problem using the same methods you've implemented in the past? Or are you willing to strive for freedom from habits and patterns to which you have become accustomed, even if it's difficult? Why is it so tempting for you to stick with "solutions" that haven't proven effective?

   _____
   _____
   _____
   _____
   _____
   _____
   _____
   _____

GOT PROBLEMS?

4. Too often, we focus on the size of our problems instead of the greatness of our God. He can change our circumstances, but He can also leave our circumstances the same and change us instead. What is the most difficult problem you face right now? Study Romans 8:35–39. What truth does the Apostle Paul share in these verses that can change your mindset about what you are facing? How can the knowledge of God's *agape* love get you through this difficult time?

_____
_____
_____
_____
_____
_____
_____
_____

5. When problems occur, we often feel alone. The good news is that no matter how lonely and isolated we feel, we are never *really* alone. Read Psalm 46:1. Describe a time when God provided refuge and strength for you while you were going through a trial. In your current circumstances, can you see how He is again providing shelter? If so, explain how. If not, ask God to reveal His provision and presence.

_____
_____
_____
_____
_____
_____
_____
_____

6. Study Proverbs 26:12 and Jeremiah 17:5–8. Does pride deter you from trusting God in your trials? If so, how?

7. When you encounter problems, do you try to avoid them? If so, what methods of avoidance do you use? Are they effective? In what ways? If they are ineffective, what could you do instead?

8. Sometimes when we face trials, we wonder whether we have offended God and the trial is a punishment that we deserve. The truth is that, while we do experience negative consequences for our foolish decisions and sin, even the most righteous people suffer unfairness and pain. Read Psalm 34:19. How does the knowledge that righteous people can have troubles affect the way you feel about your situation? How should it make us view the tribulations of others? Describe some of the ways God's deliverance might appear in your life. What are some ways He might choose to deliver you that are different from what you want?

_____
_____
_____
_____
_____
_____
_____
_____

9. Some people turn to God first when adversity comes into their lives, but others don't. They stiffen their necks and believe that they can handle their problems on their own. When adversity comes into your life, do you usually turn to God right away, or do you try to handle the problem in your own strength? If you tend to be on the side of self-reliance, what would it take for you to turn to God first?

_____
_____
_____
_____
_____
_____
_____

WHAT'S YOUR PROBLEM?

10. Jesus was able to endure the cross, and the shame that came with it, because His focus was on God. We can endure anything if we keep our focus on Jesus. Study Hebrews 12:2. When you're faced with hardship, where is your focus? If your focus is on the difficulty, what do you see and experience? If your focus is on God, what do you see and experience? If you've responded both ways, explain the difference between them and why one might be preferable to the other.

11. Sometimes we face problems because of our own bad choices or sin. Other times problems are no fault of our own. Either way, they can cause us to become bitter or develop other negative attitudes. Study Hebrews 4:12. How does this verse speak to both of these situations?

Life Application

As long as we live, we will go through different seasons. Some seasons are easier than others. If you are currently suffering heartache, you may feel that this situation will last forever. The rope of hope seems out of reach. I encourage you to look back and see how God has already worked in your life and what He's brought you through. When we look back, we can sometimes see how God was working behind the scenes. Pondering those times can help us to trust Him when we can't see what He's doing for our good *right now*.

Are you trying to handle your trials on your own? Perhaps God is waiting for you to come to the end of yourself so that you will turn to Him for help. Repent of trying to fix things in your own strength. He will forgive you and help you. If you are trusting God with your difficulties, thank Him for His love and involvement in your life.

Reflecting on the Word

"LORD, You have heard the desire of the humble;
You will prepare their heart;
You will cause Your ear to hear"
(Psalm 10:17).

∽

"Why are you cast down, O my soul?
And *why* are you disquieted within me?
Hope in God, for I shall yet praise Him
For the help of His countenance"
(Psalm 42:5).

A Reason for All Seasons

*S*everal years ago, while participating in a small-group study, we were asked to make a timeline of our lives. We started our graph with the date we were born and ended it on the day of the study. Then we were asked to mark events that occurred between those two dates that were significant to each of us. For marking purposes, we were given sticky notes of various colors, each depicting a certain event in life and its level of impact on us. When everyone had completed their timelines, there was an amazing array of colors on each person's graph.

Each of us explained our timeline to the group. There was not a dry eye in the room. As each woman shared the highs and lows of her life, we could see how those joys and sorrows had impacted her. We also witnessed the testimony of how God had worked through all the seasons of each one of our lives and how He had brought us to where we were on that day. It was amazing!

God is still active today. Let's open God's Word and continue to look for the amazing ways He works in all seasons of our lives.

1. Some Christians believe that because they are Christians, they won't face trials. Read John 16:33. What does this verse say about trials? What does Jesus tell us believers will experience? What encouragement does He give us when those times come? How can this knowledge help you when you're facing hardship?

   _____
   _____
   _____
   _____
   _____

2. King Solomon was one of the wisest and wealthiest men who ever lived, yet he wondered about the purpose of life. One of the things he realized is that there is a time and season for everything. Read Ecclesiastes 3:1–8. What can you learn from Solomon's philosophy about the seasons of life that can help you in times of difficulty?

___

3. When we experience a difficult season, we tend to ask questions like, "Why me? How long will this last? What will happen to me?" No matter what questions we have, God always has a reason for allowing even the most painful things to happen. Read Psalm 18:2, Psalm 62:2, and Psalm 62:6. What two words do these Scriptures use to describe the Lord during trials? How can knowing this truth provide comfort during hard times, even when you don't have the answers to your questions?

___

4. At times you may wonder, "What good could possibly come from this situation?" As we journey through life, we may never understand all the reasons for our afflictions. If we trust God through them, however, we can grow in our knowledge of how near He is and how much He cares. Read Psalm 34:18. Has this truth become more real to you during difficult seasons? If so, how?

   _____
   _____
   _____
   _____
   _____
   _____
   _____
   _____
   _____
   _____

5. It's never easy to experience pain and suffering, but if we grasp the depth of God's unconditional love, we can begin to trust Him more deeply. Study Ephesians 3:16–19. According to this passage, in what ways can your suffering give you a deeper understanding of God's love?

   _____
   _____
   _____
   _____
   _____
   _____
   _____
   _____
   _____

6. Sometimes God uses our suffering to accomplish a specific purpose in our lives. Other times, He uses our suffering to accomplish His purposes in the lives of others. Read Hebrews 10:24 and 2 Corinthians 1:4. Describe at least one way God might be using a trial you have experienced (or are experiencing now) to impact the life of someone else.

   _____
   _____
   _____
   _____
   _____
   _____
   _____
   _____
   _____
   _____

7. God made Jesus perfect through suffering. Jesus, who already was the perfect Son of God, completed His perfection by suffering. Read Hebrews 2:10. How might you be perfected in suffering?

   _____
   _____
   _____
   _____
   _____
   _____
   _____
   _____
   _____
   _____

8. Read Genesis 22:1–18. What does this story tell you about trust? Do you trust God's plan to make you complete? Why or why not?

9. Read Deuteronomy 4:20. With this verse in mind, what does God desire to accomplish through your trials? What are some practical steps you can take to seek God's direction during these times?

WHAT'S YOUR PROBLEM?

10. As you look back at past trials, consider how they affected you spiritually, physically, and emotionally. If you succumbed to a trial, what could you learn from that experience to prevent it from happening again? Or perhaps you actually grew from the experience. If so, how? If you did not, what steps could you take to learn something positive from the experience even now?

_____
_____
_____
_____
_____
_____
_____
_____
_____
_____

11. Read Job 23:10. During the dark time of Job's life, what did he learn about God? Describe a time when you were refined during a difficult season. If you are currently going through a trial, in what ways are you being purified?

_____
_____
_____
_____
_____
_____
_____
_____
_____
_____

12. In *What's Your Problem?* we read the testimony of Nancy, who had given up on life. God pulled her back from the brink of suicide and gave her hope where there had been none before. What impact did Nancy's story have on you? How has God spoken to you when you've felt yourself teetering at the edge of despair?

_____
_____
_____
_____
_____
_____
_____
_____
_____
_____
_____
_____

Life Application

Consider making your own timeline to help you more fully visualize how God is working in this season of life. Put it away in a safe place. When you are tempted to think He has left you (and you will be—everyone is!), go back and look at it. Remind yourself of His enduring faithfulness.

It may seem impossible to be thankful to God for all seasons, especially if you're experiencing a difficult one. But know that God is with you. He is working at this very moment. There are reasons for your struggles, and God will use them for His glory and your joy and benefit. Your timeline is not finished. It is still actively unfolding! Throughout your journey, God's presence gives your life power and purpose. Every season you experience, whether joyful or painful, will reveal the great love and grace the Father has for you.

Are you thankful for all the seasons of your life, including the difficult ones? If so, will you take a moment to thank God for working and being active in all of them? If not, will you choose to thank Him now? God wants to reveal Himself to you in new and exciting ways.

Reflecting on the Word

"And the LORD, He *is* the One who goes before you.
He will be with you, He will not leave you nor forsake you;
do not fear nor be dismayed"
(Deuteronomy 31:8).

∽

"The steps of a *good* man are ordered by the LORD,
And He delights in his way.
Though he fall, he shall not be utterly cast down;
For the LORD upholds *him with* His hand"
(Psalm 37:23–24).

Trials Aren't Wasted Time

One time when I was speaking at a conference, a woman interrupted my talk to ask a question. I answered, but my response didn't satisfy her. She kept going on and on. Her question was disruptive, and I felt that the interruption was a waste of valuable time. Even after the woman was finished, it was difficult for me to get back on track.

Not long after the conference, I shared the incident with a friend. About an hour later, she sent me a text saying that God used our discussion about the woman's question to convict her of an area of sin. After discussing the issue with her, I ended up being convicted of an area of sin in my own life as well!

Your difficulties are not a waste of time. God has a purpose for *everything* you face. Now let's not waste any time. Let's go to the Scriptures and see what the Bible says about seeming or apparent interruptions in our lives.

1. Trials have a purpose. Think of a trial that you experienced. Were you able to see that purpose while you were in the middle of the trial? Or did you only see its purpose later? How did it become clear to you? If you still don't see the purpose, how can you trust that God has a plan, even if you won't know what that plan is?

   _____
   _____
   _____
   _____
   _____
   _____

2. Often, we think of trials as having entirely negative results. Trials hurt. They exhaust us. They drain us financially, physically, emotionally, and spiritually. But now that you are on the other side of some of the trials God has brought you through, think back. Have any of them changed you for the better? If so, how? Give specific examples of how trials shaped your life, your priorities, and your character.

   _____
   _____
   _____
   _____
   _____
   _____
   _____
   _____

3. God never wastes anything. He can (and often does) turn our struggles around and use them for our good. Study 2 Corinthians 12:7–10. Paul asked God three times to remove an unnamed "thorn" from his life, but God didn't do it. What did Paul learn from that? What do you think Paul meant when he said, "When I am weak, then I am strong"? Describe how God's grace (His unearned favor) has helped you through difficult times. How has God used trials to humble you?

   _____
   _____
   _____
   _____
   _____
   _____
   _____
   _____

4. Read 2 Thessalonians 1:4. The Thessalonian church suffered persecution and trials because of their faith, and they did it with grace and confidence in God. In fact, Paul was so impressed by their steadfastness that he shared it with others. Why do you think Paul chose to include this information in his letters? How do you think the other churches responded after hearing it? Now think about your life. What kind of impact are you making on others? What kind of example are you setting?

_____
_____
_____
_____
_____
_____
_____
_____

5. Study Romans 8:28–29. What do these verses say God will do with your problems? As you face adversity, in what ways do you see yourself being conformed as described in verse 29? Now consider the response of your heart. Are you responding to God's refining hand with a willing heart or a grumbling and complaining one? What steps are you willing to take to allow God to have His way in you?

_____
_____
_____
_____
_____
_____
_____
_____

6. Have you listened to the story of someone who went through a trial and endured? Did you see a purpose in it? What was it? Did it encourage you? If so, how?

_____
_____
_____
_____
_____
_____
_____
_____
_____
_____
_____
_____

7. Study 2 Corinthians 1:3–4. Have you connected with someone who once experienced a trial similar to yours or who is experiencing a similar trial now? How did it help you to connect with that person? What did it help you learn about God's work in your life?

_____
_____
_____
_____
_____
_____
_____
_____
_____
_____
_____
_____

8. When faced with a problem, we often wonder if we have done something wrong to bring God's punishment or chastisement upon us. Read John 9:1–3. Jesus makes it clear that sometimes suffering is unrelated to our choices. According to this passage, what is one of God's purposes for our trials? When life gets hard, what lesson does God want us to learn?

   _____
   _____
   _____
   _____
   _____
   _____
   _____
   _____
   _____
   _____

9. We often find that God's plan for us is far different from what we might have chosen. Could you choose to simply yield to His plan? If so, how might that affect you? Study Romans 9:20–21. Why do you think Paul used the illustration of the potter and the clay?

   _____
   _____
   _____
   _____
   _____
   _____
   _____
   _____
   _____
   _____

10. Study Hebrews 12:6–7 (see also Proverbs 3:12). Even if you are not a parent, consider the role of discipline in helping a child learn to make good choices. Do you believe God uses discipline the same way? Why or why not?

11. When you feel out of control in a situation, how might that actually be a good thing? What good could come from that?

12. In *What's Your Problem?* we read the testimony of a woman recovering from the emotional trauma of having an abortion. Although Kim's choice was tragic, God's ability to redeem her life is encouraging, showing us how God can turn things around even for the most shattered life. What specifically encouraged you about Kim's story? Have you had a hard experience in life that has equipped you to minister to others? Explain.

_____
_____
_____
_____
_____
_____
_____
_____
_____
_____
_____
_____

Life Application

When life is enjoyable, time seems to pass quickly. However, when we experience tribulation, time seems more like a faucet that drips endlessly to the point of torture. You may not sense any purpose in what you are suffering. This lack of insight may result in feelings of relentless sadness or depression.

God is in all the details of our lives and cares deeply about what is happening to us. He has a perfect plan for each one of us, and all of our experiences are being woven into a beautiful tapestry. Are you able to trust God during the weaving process? If you struggle with trusting God, are you willing to go to Him and confess this lack of trust? Ask God to give you a proper perspective on your trials. Thank Him for providing meaning and purpose in everything you face and acknowledge that nothing you go through is wasted. Ask Him to make something beautiful from your ashes.

Reflecting on the Word

"*It is* good for me that I have been afflicted,
That I may learn Your statutes"
(Psalm 119:71).

∽

"Let us hold fast the confession of *our* hope without wavering,
for He who promised *is* faithful"
(Hebrews 10:23).

Suffering with the Right Attitude

Numerous times I have experienced problems due to my own negative attitude. Giving in to anger and depression, I have been guided by my emotions instead of God's truth. My attitude drove people away, leaving me feeling abandoned and wondering why. Changing my attitude was the answer to changing my situation. Could it be the answer for you, too? Attitude plays a big part in facing adversity. Your approach will determine your choices and the outcome.

In the midst of a trial, think about your attitude as being like a fireplace in a cold room. Like a blazing fire, a positive attitude will attract people to your warmth and the light. Like cold air blowing in from the chimney, a negative attitude will drive people away. When you face trials, are you reflecting welcoming warmth? Or negativity and distance? Let's open the Bible and see what light and warmth the Scriptures shed on our attitudes and hearts.

1. What is your attitude toward life when things are going well? Does your attitude change when you are facing a trial? Explain.

   _____
   _____
   _____
   _____
   _____
   _____
   _____

WHAT'S YOUR PROBLEM?

2. What is your attitude toward *God* when your life is going well? When you begin to face adversity, does your attitude toward Him change? If so, how?

3. Study 1 Peter 2:21–23. What kind of attitude did Jesus have when things were going well? Did His attitude change when He suffered?

SUFFERING WITH THE RIGHT ATTITUDE

4. Study James 1:2–4. How is it possible to consider it all joy when you face various trials? What difference can it make if you approach your problems with a positive attitude? According to this passage, what will result?

5. When you are faced with adversity, do you control your attitude or does your attitude control you? Explain. What course corrections can you make to change negative outlooks into positive ones?

6. When you are suffering through a trial, do you tend to place blame on someone else? If so, whom do you blame and what is your attitude toward this person? Study Romans 14:10–12 and 2 Corinthians 5:10. What do these Scriptures say about the importance of guarding our hearts against being judgmental? How might your mindset change by looking at the situation and the people involved from an eternal perspective?

7. Do you blame God for your problems? If so, how does this affect your walk with Him?

SUFFERING WITH THE RIGHT ATTITUDE

8. We may not be able to select our difficulties, but we are able to choose the attitude we take toward them. We can also choose the attitude we will take toward the people we might tend to blame. We can also choose our attitude toward God. Study Philippians 2:5. What was Jesus' attitude during the countless times He was unfairly criticized, especially by the religious leaders of His day? What about when He was so cruelly and unfairly beaten and crucified? Describe any un-Christ-like attitudes you may have in regard to difficulties. What changes are you willing to make to reflect Jesus' attitude and character?

_____
_____
_____
_____
_____
_____
_____
_____
_____
_____

9. The world's pattern in facing adversity includes thoughts like, *Why me? I don't deserve this. If God were a loving God, this wouldn't happen.* But God doesn't want us to follow the world's pattern. Study Romans 12:2. What brings renewal of your mind, allowing you to see things God's way?

_____
_____
_____
_____
_____
_____
_____
_____

WHAT'S YOUR PROBLEM?

10. When we are suffering, it can tempt us towards bitterness and anger. We can choose to give in to these emotions or we can choose to allow God to give us the strength we need and trust Him to bring good from a tough situation. Study Hebrews 12:15. What does this verse say about bitterness? Have you ever become bitter because of your trials? Explain. Who is hurt by bitterness?

_____
_____
_____
_____
_____
_____
_____
_____
_____

11. Read Exodus 16 and 32, Leviticus 24:10–16, and Numbers 12. God provided the Israelites with tremendous blessing and provision while they wandered in the desert. What was God's response when they complained? When others complain about things you have done for them, how do you feel? Does this give you insight into how God felt? Why do you think God takes grumbling so seriously? Why is there a penalty for it?

_____
_____
_____
_____
_____
_____
_____
_____
_____

12. Do you complain? (We all do it!) When you do, what do you think is your purpose for doing so? In your complaining, do you think you are being any different from the Israelites? Why or why not?

13. In *What's Your Problem?* Scott's testimony shows the healing power of God, even at the brink of death. What lessons did Scott's story teach you? Have you experienced this type of healing or know of someone who has? Explain.

Life Application

Our attitude often changes as life circumstances change. When things are good, we tend to be happy and content. When we suffer, we deteriorate into whining and negativity. We need to consider who or what we allow to control us. Is it our circumstances, our emotions, or the Holy Spirit? Choosing how we respond to adversity shows who we believe to be in control.

Consider your perspective through your struggles. Now consider the attitude necessary to honor God. Is there a difference? If you've had a poor attitude, will you go before the Lord and share that with Him? God understands how you feel, but He loves you too much to leave you there. He wants to help you reach a higher level of discernment that will give Him glory. Ask Him to give you a new outlook on your trials, then watch what He will do in and through you.

Reflecting on the Word

"I say then: Walk in the Spirit,
and you shall not fulfill the lust of the flesh.
For the flesh lusts against the Spirit,
and the Spirit against the flesh;
and these are contrary to one another,
so that you do not do the things that you wish.
But if you are led by the Spirit,
you are not under the law"
(Galatians 5:16–18).

∽

"Do all things without complaining and disputing,
that you may become blameless and harmless,
children of God without fault in the midst
of a crooked and perverse generation,
among whom you shine as lights in the world,
holding fast the word of life,
so that I may rejoice in the day of Christ
that I have not run in vain or labored in vain"
(Philippians 2:14–16).

For Such a Time as This

I occasionally enjoy visiting Dallas, Texas, where I briefly lived. One weekend, I planned to go there to rest and relax. However, when my friends learned that I would be in town, they asked me to join them for coffee and to just hang out. Although I really wanted to say no, I felt I should spend some time with them because such opportunities were rare.

It was really fun to catch up with old friends and make new ones. It wasn't long before the discussion turned to forgiving others. One woman said she had not spoken to her father in years and didn't think she could forgive him. I felt God leading me to talk with her about it. Later that evening, we sat together and talked about forgiveness. She made the decision to forgive him. When I saw her several months later, she was still experiencing freedom resulting from that decision. She had even talked with her father for the first time in years. God was healing the relationship. Had I declined the invitation that day, I wouldn't have had the opportunity to see God work in her life.

We can't always anticipate God's timing, but His Word assures us of His ongoing presence and activity in our lives. We don't need to read far in the Bible to realize that His timing is always ideal. I think this is the perfect time to open God's Word and learn what it says about His timing.

WHAT'S YOUR PROBLEM?

1. In the Old Testament, Queen Esther's life was in grave danger, yet God had a specific purpose for her unique set of circumstances. Study Esther 4:13–14. Can you think of a "for such a time as this" trial in your life when you were in the right place at the right time to fulfill God's plan? Explain.

   _____
   _____
   _____
   _____
   _____
   _____
   _____
   _____
   _____
   _____

2. King Solomon recognized, as human beings, we can only see the past and experience the present. We must trust God with the future because He is the only one who sees the whole picture from beginning to end. Read Ecclesiastes 3:11. What does this verse say to you regarding your trials? Do you believe that God guides you through the right things, to the right places, at all the right times? Why or why not?

   _____
   _____
   _____
   _____
   _____
   _____
   _____
   _____
   _____
   _____

3. We've all seen a toddler grab a toy from another child and scream, "Mine!" In the same way, we sometimes try to play tug of war with God. When our circumstances are not what we want, our hearts scream, "My way!" In our prayers, we even try to convince God to change things to suit our desires. But above all else, Jesus desired the Father's way and the Father's timing. Read Matthew 26:39 and Mark 14:36. How can you follow Jesus' example in your afflictions?

4. The world sees you on the outside, but God knows you inside and out. The world sees the problems you face, but God sees the solutions, too. God also sees the good He intends to bring from your pain. He sees not only the temporal, but also the eternal. He sees tomorrow as clearly as today. Study 2 Corinthians 4:16–18. What unseen things can you focus on during your trials? How will this help you better understand God's timing?

5. When we are facing a challenge, we often isolate ourselves rather than talking to those who could encourage us with the truth of God's Word. We need to break out of our isolation, and we often need others' help to see God's perspective instead of our own. Read Proverbs 15:22. When you go through a storm, do you hesitate to seek counsel? If so, what holds you back? What are some practical steps you can take to overcome this barrier?

___

6. God's perspective on the difficulties we face differs greatly from ours. We need to ask for help to see things through His eyes. When we do, we are more open to seeing the good that can come from our afflictions. Study Isaiah 55:8–9. Can you think of ways that your suffering could be used by God to bring you greater joy in the long run, bless someone else, or bring you or someone else closer to Christ? Explain.

___

7. Study Colossians 3:1–4. How should you view your time on earth in light of eternity? How can this perspective help you endure tough situations?

8. When faced with problems, we often try to manage our struggles on our own. However, Jesus submitted to His Father's will above all else. Study John 6:35–40 and Luke 22:42. Why do you think Jesus chose His Father's will above His, even though it meant experiencing great pain? Discern, if you can, the reason for experiencing your current trial. Does the timing have any significance? Why do you think God might have chosen this particular time for what you are going through?

9. Perhaps you know someone who is going through a time of struggle. God may have you in this person's life "for such a time as this." Read Galatians 6:2. What would this look like from the perspective of someone enduring a trial? What would it look like from the perspective of someone with a friend or acquaintance enduring one?

10. Paul and his fellow believers faced many of the same trials we face today. No matter how difficult the circumstances, however, they were not crushed. They simply continued to trust and serve Jesus. They did not despair, nor were they destroyed, because His love flowed out through them into the lives of others. They understood that they were in this place at this time for a greater purpose. Study 2 Corinthians 4:8–10. How does this passage encourage you? How can it enable you to help others?

11. God gives us opportunities to serve every day. But what if serving meant possible danger to you or someone you are close to? What if you knew it would help save someone else? Would that give you peace? How did Jesus serve in this way?

12. In *What's Your Problem?* we read the testimony of Cheryl, a woman who exhibited tremendous strength and patience throughout her marriage to an unbeliever. Cheryl agonized over her husband's rejection of Christ, but God was faithful. In the end, her husband was saved on his deathbed. How did Cheryl's story encourage you? How has God strengthened your faith as you've gone through trials?

Life Application

God brings us opportunities and opens doors to minister on a daily basis. It may be listening to people share their struggles. It may be simple acts of kindness, such as giving someone a ride to the doctor. Maybe it is revealing truth that God has given you that will speak to someone's heart at just the right time.

Unfortunately, we are often so busy and focused on our own agendas that we miss those "for such a time as this" moments. The invitation is given, but it goes by unnoticed. We have places to go, people to see, and work to get done. We focus so intently on our self-imposed tasks that we cannot hear God calling. God has prepared you for such moments to minister to His people. It's sad when we miss them. It's like spending a whole year preparing for a race, then missing the starting gun.

Are you being sensitive to the opportunities God brings into your life, even if they involve trial and suffering? If not, will you take a moment to ask Him to make you aware of those moments and use you? If so, will you thank God for those opportunities and how He has been molding you for such a time as this?

Reflecting on the Word

"See then that you walk circumspectly,
not as fools but as wise, redeeming the time,
because the days are evil.
Therefore do not be unwise,
but understand what the will of the Lord *is*"
(Ephesians 5:15–17).

༄

"As each one has received a gift,
minister it to one another,
as good stewards of the manifold grace of God.
If anyone speaks, *let him speak* as the oracles of God.
If anyone ministers, *let him do it* as with the ability which God supplies,
that in all things God may be glorified through Jesus Christ,
to whom belong the glory and the dominion forever and ever.
Amen"
(1 Peter 4:10–11).

Redefining Victory

I love playing games, especially card games. I find them particularly gratifying when I win, but of course I don't win every time I play.

Life can seem like a card game at times. It involves chance, strategy, and interactions with other players. In life, too, I like to win. I want to receive promotions and returns on investments, and I want people to approve of me. I like to feel that I have successfully invested my time and resources and have been worthy of a win. Yet I sometimes have to reevaluate my definition of winning. Is success in the world a sign of a truly victorious life? When I go through the storms of life, does that mean I can't experience victory until the storm has passed?

Jesus had no home nor worldly wealth. He had a small group of nobodies following Him, and many hated Him, especially those in authority and with social status. His ministry ended with crucifixion. His life didn't sound very victorious. Yet God made Jesus victorious in everything that really mattered. Jesus was faithful to obey His Father and to fulfill the purpose for which He was sent. In that, Jesus was the most successful person who ever lived. Because of what Jesus did, we all have victory, even in our trials if we choose it. Let's open the Bible and explore the victory that comes through Jesus Christ.

1. What does victory over a trial mean to you?

    _____
    _____
    _____
    _____
    _____
    _____
    _____

2. When faced with suffering, we often look for a simple way out rather than a successful way through. Think of a specific trial in your own life. Describe how victory *over* the trial might look. Now describe how victory *through* the trial might look.

3. Think of a "mountain" (an obstacle or trial in your life that is bigger than you have the ability to move on your own) that you are trying to climb. What would victory look like if God "moved the mountain" and changed your circumstances? How might victory look if the mountain wasn't moved and your circumstances remained the same?

4. Study John 14:27. How does God's peace differ from the world's peace? How can you experience His peace when you're going through a difficult time?

5. Another kind of victory we can experience through trials is growing in our faith. Study 1 Peter 1:6–7. What are some steps you can take to enable this to happen? Describe what you are learning right now about faith during your problems, or what you learned about faith during a problem in the past.

6. When faced with suffering, the only victory some people can see is a change in their circumstances. However, true victory is a change in our perspective. List three Scriptures or passages that help you see your trials from God's perspective rather than your own. How could this change the way you approach hardships?

_____
_____
_____
_____
_____
_____
_____
_____
_____

7. Another type of victory during a storm is simply holding on to God. The ability not to surrender is a victory in itself. Read 1 Samuel 16:7. God instructs Samuel not to consider the outside of the man, but the inside. How has God reconstructed your heart simply by the process of holding on to Him?

_____
_____
_____
_____
_____
_____
_____
_____
_____

8. When we are going through a trial, which do we often fear most? The circumstances or the God who ordained them? God wants us to fear Him—to trust Him with reverence and awe. Fearing God can also help bring us to victory in times of adversity. Look in your Bible and find five verses that discuss "fear of the Lord." What truths do you glean from them?

9. Growing in spiritual maturity is another type of victory we can experience during trials. Study Deuteronomy 8:2–3. What did God want the Israelites to learn through their experience of hunger? Have you experienced "hunger" on earth? Not necessarily for food, but for something you desperately want that has been withheld from you (marriage, children, financial security)? What could be the lessons God wants to teach you through these times?

WHAT'S YOUR PROBLEM?

10. God gives us tools to help us be victors, not victims. Study Ephesians 6:10–17. Are you wearing all of the armor God provides? Explain. Name at least one piece of armor you are wearing and describe how it helps you during adversity. Name at least one piece of armor that you should be wearing but aren't, and describe how that missing piece may be preventing you from being the victor you were designed to be.

_____
_____
_____
_____
_____
_____
_____
_____
_____

11. One of the greatest victories we can experience is enjoying God's presence, His companionship, and His love. Have you ever felt alone during a trial? Explain. How would experiencing the reality of God's love and presence change your perspective during adversity? What are some ways you can invite God into your situation?

_____
_____
_____
_____
_____
_____
_____
_____

12. In *What's Your Problem?* Kristine's testimony shows us the devastation of losing a loved one, a loss magnified by the chronic physical pain resulting from the accident. In what ways did Kristine's story speak to you in the loss of someone you love? How have you found hope, even while struggling with a burden that seems unfair?

_____
_____
_____
_____
_____
_____
_____
_____
_____
_____
_____

Life Application

Are you experiencing hardships and not feeling victorious in the midst of them? Your circumstances don't dictate whether you are living in victory or not—unless you allow them to do so. If the focus of your life is a change in your circumstances on the outside rather than a change of heart on the inside, you will be easily shaken. But even when circumstances do not change, you can choose to live in victory. You can live victoriously every day in spite of the events around you. Jesus loves you completely and wants you to experience the abundant life He has for you.

Are you experiencing victory even though you've had one trial after another? If so, thank God that victory is through Him, and Him only, and is not based on the things that happen or don't happen to you. If you feel that you are not experiencing victory, have you been trying to change your situation to feel victorious? If so, will you go to God and ask Him to change your heart? Ask Him to give you His peace in the midst of whatever you are facing. Even though you may continue to pray for a change of circumstances, a change in perspective will give you hope during the waiting process.

Reflecting on the Word

"But you have not so learned Christ,
if indeed you have heard Him and have been taught by Him,
as the truth is in Jesus:
that you put off, concerning your former conduct,
the old man which grows corrupt according to the deceitful lusts,
and be renewed in the spirit of your mind,
and that you put on the new man
which was created according to God,
in true righteousness and holiness"
(Ephesians 4:20–24).

∽

"You will keep *him* in perfect peace,
Whose mind *is* stayed *on You,*
Because he trusts in You"
(Isaiah 26:3).

Your Response Reveals Your Heart

*I*t has been said that trials do not *define* who we are. They *reveal* who we are. They do this by exposing what's really on the inside of us. They reveal the character that is already there. Have you ever known someone who was pleasant only when things were going well? Perhaps you have been present when someone felt slighted and responded with hostility. Maybe you have found your temper rising or yourself overtaken by fear when something went terribly and unexpectedly wrong.

God knows we will encounter disappointments. But He wants to use those things to make us stronger, better, and even kinder people who wholly trust and rely on Him. When we submit to God, believing He will guide us and take care of us, our response to life's challenges, even the most negative ones, will be to trust patiently. As we wait upon Him, He will refine our character and shape us into being more Christ-like. Let's start reshaping our responses to trials now by looking at God's directives in Scripture.

1. Read Romans 5:8. In response to humanity's sin problem, God gave the world Jesus. In that gift, God expressed His unfathomable love for us. But *when* did God give us this gift? When we were at our best? Or at our worst? What does this reveal about God?

   _____
   _____
   _____
   _____
   _____

2. Think about the way you respond to problems. When you are stressed, fearful, angry, or pressured, what deep character traits become exposed? What character traits would you *like* to expose?

3. When we are stressed, we tend to become reactionary. We let our circumstances dictate our responses. Have you considered that your responses can actually change the situation you find yourself in? Often, situations can have two different outcomes depending on how you respond to them. Describe how two different responses might have two entirely different outcomes in your situation. Is there one that could actually *improve* the situation? If so, which one?

4. The Apostle Paul experienced countless trials. His responses revealed a heart more focused on God's purpose than on the pain he was enduring. Study Romans 8:18. Now think of a trial you recently endured. Did you follow Paul's example? If so, how did your response of trust impact the outcome? If you did not follow his example, how might that have affected the outcome?

_____
_____
_____
_____
_____
_____
_____
_____
_____
_____

5. Read Luke 6:45. Consider how you respond to suffering (anger, complaining, giving up) and write it down. If you are responding negatively, what has to change in order for you to maintain hope, even through adversity?

_____
_____
_____
_____
_____
_____
_____
_____
_____
_____

6. Have you prayed over your difficulties, yet it seemed as if God didn't answer? What thoughts came to you during this time? What do your answers reveal about your heart?

7. What if someone else's problem had a negative impact on you? What would your response be? Include your thoughts and plan of action. Read Romans 12:14–21. Its prescription in such situations is contrary to what the world tells us to do. Would you respond to persecution or unfair blame in this biblical manner? If not, what would need to change in order for you to do so?

YOUR RESPONSE REVEALS YOUR HEART

8. Our perspective can make a tremendous difference in the way we respond to problems. Are we Christ-focused or self-focused? Study Philippians 3:7–11. How does this passage describe the difference between these two approaches? How should this affect your responses?

   _____
   _____
   _____
   _____
   _____
   _____
   _____
   _____
   _____
   _____

9. Study Galatians 5:22–23. In difficult times, are you able to reflect at least some of the spiritual fruit given to you? Explain. How would your life change if you allowed God to truly develop these traits in you?

   _____
   _____
   _____
   _____
   _____
   _____
   _____
   _____
   _____
   _____

10. Paul's ministry took him through times of both wonderful fellowship and extreme suffering and danger. Sometimes he had abundant material blessings. Other times he had very few. At times he walked in physical freedom. Other times he spent long years in prison. Study Philippians 4:11–13. How did Paul respond to the comfortable situations? How about the uncomfortable ones? How was he able to do this? How can you follow Paul's example and learn to be content even in the most difficult circumstances?

_____
_____
_____
_____
_____
_____
_____
_____
_____

11. List three Bible characters whom you admire for their godly responses during times of affliction. What character traits did they display that you would like to exhibit in your own life? What steps can you take to allow those traits to blossom?

_____
_____
_____
_____
_____
_____
_____
_____

YOUR RESPONSE REVEALS YOUR HEART

12. In *What's Your Problem?* we read of the miracle God performed in David's life, ridding him of his addiction to meth and strengthening him to minister to others with addictions. Addictions can not only be to physical substances like drugs and alcohol, but also to unhealthy habits such as viewing pornography, shopping, and gambling. What does this miracle tell you about the power of God over all types of addictions?

_____
_____
_____
_____
_____
_____
_____
_____
_____
_____

Life Application

The real test of character occurs during times of trial. Difficulties show what we are made of and where our dependence really lies. Are we standing on a strong foundation of faith or are we floundering knee deep in doubt? God promises to uphold us and help us through all of our troubles as we trust Him and build our lives upon the solid rock of His Word.

How have you responded to the challenges you've faced? In the process of studying this material, maybe you were surprised by what you learned about yourself and the way you handle trials. Do your coping mechanisms need to change in order to better honor God? If you are reacting negatively, are you ready to admit that your response isn't what it should be? Will you allow God to give you a tender heart of obedience? Tell God you're ready to respond to your trials in a way that honors Him. Trust God to get you to the place you need to be.

Reflecting on the Word

"Having eyes, do you not see?
And having ears, do you not hear?
And do you not remember?"
(Mark 8:18).

༄

"Examine yourselves *as to* whether you are in the faith.
Test yourselves.
Do you not know yourselves,
that Jesus Christ is in you?
—unless indeed you are disqualified"
(2 Corinthians 13:5).

When We Don't Understand

Scripture says that God causes all things to work together for good for those who love Him and are called according to His purpose (Romans 8:28). As Christians, circumstances are not random or useless in God's hands. If you look under the hood of a vehicle, you will see pipes, belts, tanks, and other components. Every part, whether small or large, serves a vital purpose that enables the vehicle to operate. You may not understand how each component works, but the engineer who designed it does—and knows that each piece is critical.

In the same way, you might look at the parts and the pieces of your life (including your past) and be unsure how they work together. You might wonder how each element will impact the future God has planned for you. Thankfully, we don't have to understand it all. We can trust that God, the designer of our souls, bodies, and hearts, knows how to cause all things to work together for good. He doesn't require us to master the subject or to take charge, but rather to have faith in Him, even when we don't understand. Let's go to God's Word for more insight and greater peace, even when we don't understand the reason behind the challenges we face.

1. When faced with a problem, sometimes we struggle to understand the reason for it. Have you ever experienced this struggle? Explain.

    _____
    _____
    _____
    _____
    _____

WHAT'S YOUR PROBLEM?

2. Read Psalm 55:22. Think back to a time when you were weighed down with a problem, trying to understand it. Did you cast that care on the Lord? If you did, describe the results. What happened to your need to understand? If you didn't cast your cares on the Lord, what steps can you take to do it next time? What does this verse say will happen if you do?

   _____
   _____
   _____
   _____
   _____
   _____
   _____
   _____
   _____
   _____

3. God wants us to trust Him, even when we don't understand the reasons for our suffering. Study Proverbs 3:5–6. If most of your thoughts have centered on trying to understand the "whys" of your pain, describe steps you can take to stop trying to figure it all out and simply trust God instead. What are some practical measures you can take to acknowledge Him as you go through trials?

   _____
   _____
   _____
   _____
   _____
   _____
   _____
   _____
   _____

4. In the midst of a trial, perhaps all you can see is the pain. God may seem very far away. However, God doesn't tell us to navigate life's journey based on what we can see. Study 2 Corinthians 5:7. What does the Bible say is guiding our steps as we walk through life? Where are we to put our eyes? What would it look like for you to live according to this principle more often?

   _____
   _____
   _____
   _____
   _____
   _____
   _____
   _____
   _____
   _____

5. Trials often result from the natural human responses of worry and anxiety. Because we don't understand the reasons why we suffer, we often struggle to make sense of our circumstances. Study Philippians 4:6–7. When we cannot control the circumstances around us (much less make sense of them), what does this passage tell us to do? If we obey God's teaching, what does He promise will result? Describe a time when you found this to be true in your life.

   _____
   _____
   _____
   _____
   _____
   _____
   _____
   _____
   _____
   _____

WHAT'S YOUR PROBLEM?

6. Why do you think God doesn't allow us to know everything?

   _____
   _____
   _____
   _____
   _____
   _____
   _____
   _____
   _____
   _____
   _____

7. Read Genesis 3. The desire to understand everything goes back to the Garden of Eden and the temptation created by the tree of knowledge of good and evil. We know Adam and Eve sinned by eating the fruit, but what was the other sin committed? Why do you think this is?

   _____
   _____
   _____
   _____
   _____
   _____
   _____
   _____
   _____
   _____
   _____

WHEN WE DON'T UNDERSTAND

8. There is nothing in the Bible that tells us that, in itself, acquiring knowledge is wrong. In fact, the Bible praises and encourages the pursuit of wisdom. At what point can the desire to understand become a spiritual problem and why?

9. Read Psalm 53:2. When faced with difficult situations, what does this verse say about how to gain understanding?

WHAT'S YOUR PROBLEM?

10. God loves us and wants what is best for us. In our natural minds, we tend to think that this means avoiding trials and suffering altogether. (Think about how much time you spend asking God to take your problems away!) But God knows that sometimes it is best for us to endure suffering. Study Job 2:10. What did Job say we should accept along with the good in life? Why do you think he said that?

_____
_____
_____
_____
_____
_____
_____
_____
_____

11. Jesus did not promise us a life without pain, but He did promise things that are even better. He promised His presence, His help, His strength, and His healing power. Read Psalm 147:3. Describe a time when Jesus healed your wounds. Did you see it as healing at the time? Or did you only come to see it later? Explain.

_____
_____
_____
_____
_____
_____
_____
_____
_____

12. In *What's Your Problem?* we read the testimony of Kirk and his wife. Their loss of an unborn child was heart-wrenching, yet God blessed them for their faithfulness by blessing them with other children. Have you experienced loss after loss in your own life? Were you tempted to lose heart? What strength can you draw from Kirk's story?

_____
_____
_____
_____
_____
_____
_____
_____
_____
_____

Life Application

Many events in this world don't make sense. When we hear that a pilot intentionally crashes a plane into a mountainside, killing everyone on board, or when we hear of a brutal mass beheading by an extremist rebel group, we are shaken to the core. As we watch unfathomable events unfold around us, we can feel helpless and small. We can feel very alone. But Scripture says that, no matter how bad things get or how scary they seem, God never leaves us nor forsakes us (Hebrews 13:5).

Have you felt angry because you didn't understand the painful things you were going through? Maybe God didn't answer your prayers in the way you wanted or within the time frame you expected. If that's your reaction, do you realize what you are really saying? You are saying that you know better than God! If you have given up on God, how has that worked for you in the past? Acknowledge your need for God, including His ways and His timing. This will result in a growing relationship with Him. Actively desire and seek His presence and follow His wisdom, even when He takes you down a path different from the one you would have chosen. God will comfort you in ways you've never imagined.

Reflecting on the Word

"This *is* my comfort in my affliction,
For Your word has given me life"
(Psalm 119:50).

∽

"*Which is* manifest evidence of the righteous judgment of God,
that you may be counted worthy of the kingdom of God,
for which you also suffer;
since *it is* a righteous thing with God
to repay with tribulation those who trouble you,
and to *give* you who are troubled rest with us
when the Lord Jesus is revealed
from heaven with His mighty angels"
(2 Thessalonians 1:5–7).

Forks in the Road

When it comes to trials, we always have decisions to make, even if they are simply what our attitudes will be. I remember a time when being in a conflict with someone brought me to a fork in the road where I had to ask myself, *Am I going to remain bitter and not talk to this person or am I going to forgive, go to the person, confess my wrong, and make things right?* If I want to make the right decision, the critical question is always, *Which decision lines up with Scripture?* Emotionally, I didn't want to make things right at the time. But I chose to lay my emotions aside and reconcile. Today, my relationship with that person is better and stronger than ever.

What about you? What spiritual decisions do you currently face? We can either be guided by our feelings or find the right direction by searching God's truths. Let's choose to find our answers in Scripture now.

1. Sometimes our problems are not of our own making. A town is hit by a natural disaster. Someone chooses to drive drunk and causes an accident. Other times, our problems are a direct result of our own choices, such as the lifestyle we choose. Are you able to connect any of your past problems to your choices? Not a lot can be done about old mistakes, except learning the lesson, but if you are currently making bad choices, it's not too late to correct them. What are some of your choices that could use some course correction right now? How can you involve God in the process?

   _____
   _____
   _____
   _____
   _____

2. When you are in the midst of suffering, how can your faith help you and what specifically can you pray about as you wait for God's solution?

3. When we are experiencing the stress and pain of a trial, decision-making can be difficult. But God promises never to leave us alone. He promises to stand by us and "uphold us with His righteous right hand." Read Isaiah 41:10. In the Bible, the "right hand of God" refers to His ultimate power. To be upheld by God's right hand means being sustained by this unfathomable, limitless power. How could you apply the truth of this verse to the choices you are facing right now?

FORKS IN THE ROAD

4. Sometimes God allows us to face trials because He wants to bring about change in our lives. Perhaps we have become complacent. Perhaps we are too comfortable where we are, and God wants to move us in a new direction. While a trial may be uncomfortable, it may be the best way to get us to move. Could God be using your circumstances to move you in a new direction? How could the problems you are experiencing force you to make a choice that will move you to a new place God has planned for you? Without these circumstances, do you think you would get to that place on your own? Explain.

   _____
   _____
   _____
   _____
   _____
   _____
   _____

5. When we are faced with adversity, we often feel alone, especially when we have decisions to make. But God desires to generously give wisdom to anyone who asks for it in faith. Study James 1:5–6. Have you ever tried to figure things out without seeking God's wisdom? Describe the result. How about a time when you did ask God for wisdom but continued worrying anyway? Or kept trying to make decisions on your own? What happened then? Now describe a time when you trusted God alone for the answer. How was it different?

   _____
   _____
   _____
   _____
   _____
   _____
   _____

6. Do you ever get tired of doing the right thing and feeling that you never reap any benefits? Maybe you are always doing nice things for others, doing what you think God is calling you to do, but you still seem to have one problem after another. Study Galatians 6:7–10. How can this passage encourage you in such situations?

7. Often the choices we make seem right at first, but they end up leading us into pitfalls. Study Proverbs 14:12 (see also Proverbs 16:25). Have there been times when you were sure you made a wise choice only to discover later that you'd actually made a foolish one? What were the consequences? How did God display His grace to you in that situation?

8. Decision-making can be challenging in the best of times. When we are in the midst of a storm, it can seem overwhelming. Do you ever pray for direction and guidance, only to be besieged by doubt and confusion? Does decision-making become impossible because you are paralyzed by the fear of making the wrong choice? Study Hebrews 12:1. What does this verse say about such things?

_____
_____
_____
_____
_____
_____
_____
_____
_____
_____

9. God does not always expect us to have the perfect answer. He does call us to always have faith in Him. Study Romans 4:5. Even if you were to make the wrong choice in a situation, do you believe it hinders His ability to work? Does it limit His power? Explain. How can knowing this free up your ability to make decisions?

_____
_____
_____
_____
_____
_____
_____
_____
_____
_____

WHAT'S YOUR PROBLEM?

10. There are times when we need help making decisions during trials, but we don't know where to turn. We might feel as if the problem is too insignificant to take to God. We may feel unworthy to ask for His help or feel that perhaps He doesn't care. God wants us to turn to Him with all of our problems, even the little ones. When we do, the Bible promises us His mercy and grace. Read Hebrews 4:16. In what ways does this verse encourage you to seek His help?

    _____
    _____
    _____
    _____
    _____
    _____
    _____
    _____

11. In *What's Your Problem?* Aleta shared her story of being adopted and then losing her adoptive parents in a plane crash. Alcohol and drugs led her and her boyfriend down a path of addiction. When they hit rock bottom, however, both turned to God. They married and now minister to others trapped in addiction. What parts of Aleta's story spoke to you? Describe a time in your own life when you turned to God after hitting rock bottom.

    _____
    _____
    _____
    _____
    _____
    _____
    _____
    _____

Life Application

Life is full of choices. If we consider all the choices we make during a day, it is mind-boggling. At times, choices can lead us in distinctly different directions. Although we may want to do the right things, we don't always know which way to go. From a human perspective, sometimes the choices to which God is calling us may appear to make things worse. Ask God to let you see through His eyes. Learn to stop and spend time with God in consultation and submission. This quiet time is crucial to making good choices, especially during times of suffering.

If you have been relying on your own thoughts and experiences rather than God's ultimate wisdom, will you repent of that? Are you willing to tell God that you desperately need the wisdom that only He can give? Once you do that, you will find that He will be faithful to guide you. He is always ready to hear your prayer.

Reflecting on the Word

"Show me Your ways, O Lord;
Teach me Your paths.
Lead me in Your truth and teach me,
For You *are* the God of my salvation;
On You I wait all the day"
(Psalm 25:4–5).

∽

"Who *is* wise and understanding among you?
Let him show by good conduct *that* his works
are done in the meekness of wisdom.
But if you have bitter envy and self-seeking in your hearts,
do not boast and lie against the truth.
This wisdom does not descend from above,
but *is* earthly, sensual, demonic.
For where envy and self-seeking *exist,*
confusion and every evil thing *are* there"
(James 3:13–16).

Muscle-Building Adversity

When I started running several years ago, I would begin with a run-walk pattern for a couple of miles. This worked well until I woke up one morning with excruciating pain in my calf muscles. My body was letting me know that it had had enough and needed to rest. I also learned that I needed to stretch more and drink more water. I'm not giving up. My goal is to be able to run free of pain and for longer distances. Through the challenges, I learned more and will become a better runner.

The Christian life can be like that, too. We read our Bibles and pray in order to strengthen our spiritual muscles. Then something happens that seems to knock the wind out of us. It is during these times that we learn and get stronger. Talk to someone who has been through a difficult journey and ask how it has changed their life for the better. There are many examples in Scripture that show how people came through challenges and became stronger, too. Let's gain strength for our challenges through the words of the Bible.

1. When times are good in your life, how do you grow spiritually?

   _____
   _____
   _____
   _____
   _____
   _____
   _____
   _____

2. When you are faced with hardship, how do you grow spiritually?

3. God is at work in every believer's life. He began a good work in you when you trusted in Christ, and He will continue to help you grow. Study Philippians 1:6. When do you grow the most spiritually? When things are running smoothly? Or during challenging circumstances? Why do you think this is?

MUSCLE-BUILDING ADVERSITY

4. Have you found that the growth you experienced in one trial prepared you for another? Explain.

5. The Bible doesn't say that believers will never suffer. But God does promise that, after we have suffered a little while, He will restore, confirm, strengthen, and establish us. Study 1 Peter 5:10. How does God use suffering to build you up and restore you?

6. When you experience adversity, do you reflect more of God or more of yourself? If you are reflecting more of yourself than God, why do you think that is? What steps can you take to allow God to change you from the inside out?

   _____
   _____
   _____
   _____
   _____
   _____
   _____
   _____
   _____
   _____
   _____

7. Study 1 Thessalonians 5:16–18 (see also Ephesians 5:20). How can "rejoicing always, praying continually, and giving thanks in all circumstances" bring about change? Where is that change occurring? What are some results you might expect?

   _____
   _____
   _____
   _____
   _____
   _____
   _____
   _____
   _____
   _____
   _____

MUSCLE-BUILDING ADVERSITY

8. We can rejoice in our sufferings if we realize that suffering produces endurance, which produces character, which produces hope. No matter how big our problems might be, they can present opportunities for growth. Study Romans 5:3–5. When problems arise, what positive traits can result from your obedience to God? Think back to the hard times you have experienced in the past or a problem you are living through now. How did God use your struggles to produce good spiritual fruit?

_____
_____
_____
_____
_____
_____
_____
_____
_____
_____

9. People change, circumstances change, and we as individuals change. Some changes can bring confusion or insecurity, especially when we face difficulty. Read Hebrews 13:8. How can knowing that Jesus never changes strengthen you in difficult times?

_____
_____
_____
_____
_____
_____
_____
_____

10. In Genesis 37–45, Joseph's brothers were jealous of him and sold him into slavery. After he was wrongly accused of attacking Potiphar's wife, he was thrown into prison. Despite continual disappointments, God was with him. Joseph made the best of every situation and grew in wisdom and godly character. Ultimately, God used these circumstances for good—to save His chosen people from the coming famine. Read Genesis 50:20. What did Joseph tell his brothers after he was reunited with them? Do you see any parallels with your own life? Have you experienced a rough road, where it seemed that someone else benefitted at your expense? Has this experience led you to stronger faith, more Christ-likeness, greater compassion, or some other eternal benefit? Explain.

MUSCLE-BUILDING ADVERSITY

11. God often uses His Word to rebuke or correct His children. Regularly reading the Bible and memorizing verses or passages can equip us to deal with trials when we are in the midst of them. Study 2 Timothy 3:16–17. What lessons can Scripture teach you when you're faced with adversity? How might God use His Word to rebuke or correct you in the midst of your struggle? How can the Bible train and equip you to deal with your anguish? Describe a time when the Scriptures helped you with a problem. What verse or verses encouraged you in affliction?

12. In *What's Your Problem?* Mike's testimony demonstrates the grace and compassion God shows His people, even when they rebel to follow an ungodly lifestyle. How do you see God's compassion displayed in Mike's story of redemption? How has He shown you grace and compassion when you've turned your back on Him?

Life Application

Sometimes God allows us to face a time of adversity that feels painful but serves to make us stronger. Your life experiences might feel like running on a treadmill. You might feel as if you are laboring to move forward—that you are working hard, experiencing pain in the process, but aren't making progress. Be encouraged. No season lasts forever. While you are pressing forward, you are growing stronger. Don't resist the lessons you are learning.

As you give your problems to God and choose to rest on His promises, He will build your character and strengthen your faith. As you grow, you can testify to the goodness of God and encourage others.

Do you feel weak and weary when you face adversity? If so, now is the time to go to God and enter His rest. Ask Him how He wants to strengthen and mature you through your challenges. Thank God for using your struggles to make you stronger.

Reflecting on the Word

"Have you not known? Have you not heard?
The everlasting God, the LORD,
The Creator of the ends of the earth,
Neither faints nor is weary.
His understanding is unsearchable.
He gives power to the weak,
And to *those who have* no might He increases strength.
Even the youths shall faint and be weary,
And the young men shall utterly fall,
But those who wait on the LORD
Shall renew *their* strength;
They shall mount up with wings like eagles,
They shall run and not be weary,
They shall walk and not faint"
(Isaiah 40:28–31).

༄

"And when they had preached the gospel to that city and made many disciples, they returned to Lystra, Iconium, and Antioch, strengthening the souls of the disciples, exhorting *them* to continue in the faith, and *saying,* 'We must through many tribulations enter the kingdom of God'"
(Acts 14:21–22).

Want Hope? Stop, Drop, and Roll

There was a season in my life when I really struggled with depression. I no longer remember all the details of what I was dealing with, but I do remember that I was very circumstance-controlled instead of Spirit-controlled. I felt as if the walls were closing in on me as I fell headlong into a pit. Inside the hole, everything looked dark and I saw no way out. I felt there was no hope. Looking through my human eyes, all I could see was darkness. But as I began to take my eyes off my circumstances and look up, then I saw the light of hope.

God has the answer for you. He can easily reach inside the pit and rescue you, although the process is not always short or simple. Sometimes He doesn't rescue us right away because there are things we must go through as we grow in our spiritual walks. God knows and understands what each of us encounters. At times, His answer may come quickly. Other times, you will have to wait. Whatever the case, you can experience God's peace and the comfort of His presence in the midst of your turmoil. Sometimes it's hard to keep walking in your Christian faith, but there is always light above, and there is always hope. Let's find the hope God has to offer in the living Word.

1. When you face adversity, is Jesus your hope? This can be easy to say, but it may or may not be the way we live our lives. Is Jesus *really* your hope? If so, describe how. If not, what is preventing you from allowing Him to be?

   _____
   _____
   _____
   _____
   _____

WHAT'S YOUR PROBLEM?

2. Many times, we try to carry burdens we were not meant to carry. Jesus loves you and wants to lift the weight of your trials. He doesn't promise a carefree life, but He does promise to bear the load of your troubles. In doing so, He promises to replace your weariness and stress with rest and peace. However, even after we've laid down our burdens, it's all too easy to go back and pick them up again. Study Matthew 11:28–30. What would it take for you to lay your burdens at Jesus' feet—and leave them there? What would it look like for you to take His yoke upon you and enter into His rest?

3. Thinking about positive things may not change your circumstances, but it will change the way you deal with them. Study Philippians 4:8. Make a list of people and things in your life that are noble, right, pure, lovely, admirable, excellent, and praiseworthy. How can this list help as you face problems?

WANT HOPE? STOP, DROP, AND ROLL

4. Going through a difficult trial can produce a churning cauldron of negative thoughts and feelings such as fear, depression, and hopelessness. During these times, we may feel so overwhelmed that we don't think we can make it through. Read Isaiah 43:2. How do these promises speak to your thoughts and feelings when you're facing adversity? How can they give you hope when things seem hopeless?

   _____
   _____
   _____
   _____
   _____
   _____
   _____
   _____
   _____
   _____

5. It's easy to lose hope when our problems persist for long seasons. We try to come up with every possible solution, and ultimately we may conclude that a positive outcome is impossible. Study Matthew 19:26 and Luke 1:37. How can these Scriptures give you hope during trials?

   _____
   _____
   _____
   _____
   _____
   _____
   _____
   _____
   _____
   _____

WHAT'S YOUR PROBLEM?

6. Sometimes our problems are the result of a direct attack from our enemy, the devil. When that happens, the first step in regaining hope is recognizing the problem as an attack. Read James 4:7. What two steps does this Scripture direct you to take? What does it promise will happen if you do? In your specific situation, list several ways you can submit yourself to God. List several ways to resist the devil.

   _____
   _____
   _____
   _____
   _____
   _____
   _____
   _____
   _____
   _____

7. Even though the devil wants to destroy us, Jesus promises to give us a rich and satisfying life. Read John 10:10. What hope do you find in these words of Jesus?

   _____
   _____
   _____
   _____
   _____
   _____
   _____
   _____
   _____
   _____

8. If we trust God through our life experiences, even the most troubling times can become the foundation for a stronger and more mature faith. Read Psalm 71:20. Describe a time when God restored you and lifted you up after a difficult trial. How does remembering that help you now?

   _____
   _____
   _____
   _____
   _____
   _____
   _____
   _____
   _____
   _____
   _____

9. When you are struggling with a problem, where do you turn for help? Who has helped you in the past? On whom can you depend? Study Psalm 121. How can this Psalm comfort you in difficult times?

   _____
   _____
   _____
   _____
   _____
   _____
   _____
   _____
   _____
   _____
   _____

10. No matter what struggles we face, nothing and nobody can change who we are in Christ. Read 2 Corinthians 5:17. How should your identity in Christ impact the way you approach your struggles?

11. Study 1 Corinthians 13:13. What is the correlation between faith and hope?

12. Pornography has a tight grip on many people. In *What's Your Problem?* Eddie shares how God freed him from addiction to porn and reconciled him to his family. How did Eddie's story encourage you? Is there—or has there ever been—a sin in your life with a tight grip on you? Explain..

___
___
___
___
___
___
___
___
___
___
___
___

Life Application

Maybe you are experiencing a trial and feel as if you've fallen into a pit and can't get out. You are hungry for freedom, feeling hurt and isolated. Any options you thought were out there are gone, and darkness overshadows your life. You are losing hope that God knows and cares because your trial has gone on so long. Talk to God about it. Stop trying to figure out how you got into the pit and focus on how to get out instead. Look up instead of focusing on what's going on around you.

Are you fearful? If so, confess your fear and lack of faith. Ask God to fill you anew with hope as you take Him at His Word. As you do, you will find rest, peace, love, and joy in Him. The blessings of God are waiting for you.

Reflecting on the Word

"Yea, though I walk through the valley
 of the shadow of death,
I will fear no evil;
For You *are* with me;
Your rod and Your staff,
they comfort me"
(Psalm 23:4).

∽

"Bless the Lord, O my soul,
 And forget not all His benefits:
Who forgives all your iniquities,
Who heals all your diseases,
Who redeems your life from destruction,
Who crowns you with lovingkindness and tender mercies,
Who satisfies your mouth with good *things,*
So that your youth is renewed like the eagle's.
The Lord executes righteousness
And justice for all who are oppressed"
(Psalm 103:2–6).

12

Enduring with Patience

One summer, I went to an arts festival where I saw a huge pen drawing of a Native American chief. It was about the size of a wall mural, and from a distance it appeared to be a traditional drawing. But as I drew closer, I saw something fascinating. The image was actually created from thousands of little dots. The closer I got, the more visible the dots became. At the same time, the larger image disappeared. At a certain point, I was so close that the entire mural seemed to be nothing more than a maze of dots. When I backed up, the entire image became crisp and clear again. I wondered about the making of that unique drawing. The artist must have had to regularly step back in the process to see how his work was taking shape. I cannot imagine the patience it took to create such a masterpiece, but the result was beautiful.

Our lives sometimes feel like a work of thousands of dots. From our human perspective, our circumstances feel disjointed and random, especially during challenges. We ache to see the larger, more cohesive picture, but we lack a broad and eternal perspective. The process of God's work in us often seems so slow and disjointed that nothing beautiful will ever result. Depression can set in as we focus on what seems to be a hopeless situation. However, we can be sure that, like the artist who drew the Native American chief, God ensures that each point in our lives connects in His larger plan.

God is a master artist. His work in our lives is perfect, even if we sometimes find it hard to be patient or cannot see the bigger picture. Let's apply Scriptures to better understand His artistic strokes on the canvases of our lives.

WHAT'S YOUR PROBLEM?

1. How can trials teach us patience? What is required on our end to learn patience during these times?

2. Study Lamentations 3:25. Where does this verse tell us to focus as we wait? What or whom should we seek? How will that help us be more patient?

3. We can increase our body strength through physical exercise. We can increase our patience by exercising our faith. Could that be one reason for trials? Read Romans 12:12. Describe a time when you learned (or did not learn) patience through tribulation.

   _____
   _____
   _____
   _____
   _____
   _____
   _____
   _____
   _____
   _____

4. When we are experiencing a trial, whether in the aggravation of day-to-day living or in a time of crisis, we can be influenced by many forces. We may even feel pulled to please certain people out of fear of rejection. We may also feel compelled to respond to pressures (whether real or imagined) rather than waiting on God. Study Galatians 1:10. What answer does this verse give us for these situations? Share a time when you sought man's approval instead of God's. What was the result?

   _____
   _____
   _____
   _____
   _____
   _____
   _____
   _____
   _____

5. Read Romans 8:24–25. How do you see patience and hope blending together to form faith in your trials?

6. Study James 1:12. When you are in the midst of a struggle, what is your initial response? Do you seek to persevere through the situation, or do you seek an exit? Explain. What are the blessings of persevering through a trial?

7. When we are experiencing a problem, certain things often need to happen before God brings about the solution. Perhaps we need to make different choices, have a change of attitude, or just trust God to bring about good from the circumstances, whether in our lives or the lives of others. Study James 5:7–8. How do these verses apply to the suffering you may be experiencing? How can this help you endure more patiently?

___

8. In our rush-rush, hurry-up, instant-gratification world, we can find it difficult to wait for anything, especially during times of trouble. Yet patience is sometimes our only option. The Bible calls this *longsuffering*. Read Psalm 27:14. Where should your attention be during periods of longsuffering? How can God give you the strength to wait patiently?

___

WHAT'S YOUR PROBLEM?

9. In the Old Testament, David patiently endured all the years Saul sought to kill him. He placed his faith in God and never wavered. Study Psalm 40:1–3. Describe four ways God blessed David for his faithfulness. How has God blessed you (or someone you know) during times of adversity? Does this help you see your trials differently? If so, how?

10. What is the correlation between faith and patience? Can you develop patience as a character trait without faith? Explain.

11. How might patience help you endure your problems? How might enduring adversity help you develop more patience?

___

12. In *What's Your Problem?* my testimony of being healed from cancer without chemo or radiation has encouraged many people facing similar situations. What did my testimony show you about the love and power of God in scary situations?

___

Life Application

Waiting patiently can be a tremendous challenge, especially during times of trial. Most of us do not like waiting, and we aren't very good at it. We see waiting as wasted time. To be more efficient, we try to call the shots and control the timing of events around us. This can lead to internal conflict with regard to trusting God. But when we finally stop trying to dictate to God when and what should happen next, He can move in ways we've never imagined.

Is it time to ask God to take over and help you endure with patience? Waiting has its own rewards. New strength, courage, and hope for the future can be gained as you face your trials and endure patiently through them.

Reflecting on the Word

"Rest in the LORD, and wait patiently for Him;
Do not fret because of him who prospers in his way,
Because of the man who brings wicked schemes to pass"
(Psalm 37:7).

∽

"My brethren, take the prophets,
who spoke in the name of the Lord,
as an example of suffering and patience.
Indeed we count them blessed who endure.
You have heard of the perseverance of Job
and seen the end *intended by* the Lord—
that the Lord is very compassionate and merciful"
(James 5:10–11).

Conclusion

As you come to the end of this study guide, I hope this information has encouraged you to take an important step toward a new direction. God is always available, and He wants to transform your life.

I hope that as you carefully considered each question, you discovered better ways of responding to life's challenges. The principles in this study guide are the ones I use in my counseling practice, principles that have changed people's perspectives on trials and tribulation. These truths are not my own; they are found in God's Word. The God who created us understands exactly how we feel, how we operate, and how we respond to difficult situations.

Because God loves us with deep compassion, it is His greatest desire to teach us how to rise above our circumstances and live full and fruitful lives. I pray that God will use these truths to reveal Himself and His plan as you draw near to Him. Learn to lean on His wisdom instead of your own. It is my desire that you experience peace and joy as you apply these eternal precepts because God is good and His mercy endures forever (Psalm 118:1).

About the Author

*D*r. Emily Edwards is an emerging voice of hope within the field of Christian counseling. She is a bright, positive, and informed writer and speaker who spends much of her time counseling and helping others in the pursuit, development, and implementation of long-term, meaningful relationships. She frequently travels around the United States and overseas, leading seminars and retreats for singles, women, and married couples. Edwards received her Ph.D. in Christian counseling from Vision International University in 2002, along with certifications in pastoral counseling and marriage and family counseling. In 2015, Edwards received her Masters in biblical counseling from Victorious Christian Life Institute. The scope of her work and ministry includes personal counseling, teaching biblical principles on the storms of life, relationships, forgiveness, and recovery for the hurting.

Notes

Notes

Notes

Notes

Notes

www.ingramcontent.com/pod-product-compliance
Lightning Source LLC
LaVergne TN
LVHW081354060426
835510LV00013B/1817